Winter 2022

QUARTERLY BOOK MAGAZINE
ISSUE 01

Review Tales
A Book Magazine For Indie Authors

Happy Holidays!
START THE YEAR READING WHAT YOU LOVE

Author *Confessions*
Things I should have known!

Editor's Picks
BOOKS TO READ IN THE NEW YEAR

10 Insightful BOOK REVIEWS

WORDS OF WISDOM
FROM THE WRITING COMMUNITY

Winter 2022

**QUARTERLY BOOK MAGAZINE
ISSUE 01**

Review Tales
A Book Magazine For Indie Authors

Happy Holidays!

START THE YEAR READING
WHAT YOU LOVE

Author
Confessions

Things I should have known!

Editor's Picks
BOOKS TO READ IN THE NEW YEAR

10 Insightful
BOOK REVIEWS

WORDS OF WISDOM
FROM THE WRITING COMMUNITY

Review Tales
A Book Magazine For Indie Authors

COPYRIGHT © 2022
Review Tales Magazine - A Book Magazine for Indie Authors
This magazine may not be reproduced, either in part or in its entirety, in any form, by any means, without written permission from the publisher, with the exception of brief excerpts for purposes of radio, television, or published review. Although all possible means have been taken to ensure the accuracy of the material presented, Review Tales is not liable for any misinterpretation, misapplication or typographical errors.
All rights, including the right of translation, are reserved.
Founder & Editor in Chief: S. Jeyran Main
Publisher: Review Tales Publishing & Editing Services
Print & distribution: Ingram Spark
Cover Photo: Melike benli
Designs: Pexels
ISBN 978-1-988680-12-5 (paper)
ISBN 978-1-988680-13-2 (digital)
www.jeyranmain.com
For all inquiries please contact us directly.

Contributors

Serena Agusto-Cox: Poetic Book Tours
C A Deegan: What to do when it's all new!
Rod A. Walters: What do you do with a drunk-en writ-er's block?
Dennis Scheel: Author confessions
Steven Day: Of politics and fiction
Mary Ann V. Mercer, Psy.D.
Radhika Iyer
Steve Stephenson and K.M. Tedrick
E. Prybylski
Josie Allen
Dovydas Klimavičius
J. Lyndon Hickman
Anthology of short stories forwarded by Dan Fogler
Ashley B. Venenga
Rob Samborn
Boshra Rasti: Piercing words
Rojé Augustin: Words of wisdom
Louise Bélanger: Finding your audience
Robert Bossler: Relating to wonder
Rob Samborn: Thinking outside the box
George Pallas: The power of your peers
Brett Atlas: Creating something meaningful
Siobhán O'Regan
Kate Peters
Caroline Clemens
Jill Reid
Greg Rajaram
Neil Perry Gordon
Michael Backus
Bruce Calhoun
Dylan Madeley
Allison Hong Merrill

Photo Credits from Pexels:
Cottonbro p.2
Dzenina Lukac p.22
Hissetmehurriyeti p.i
Küflü çıkın p.2
Ykanite Koppens p.22
Ena Marinkovic p.30

Special thanks to:
Gina Burby
Vaughn Stelzenmuller
Christopher Main
S. M. A. Boutorabi
Fatemeh S. Fard

Contents

01 Editor's Note

02 Author Confessions

11 Ten Book Reviews

22 Author Words of Wisdom

30 Author Interview

37 Editor's Pick

39 Starred Books

Editor's Note

Welcome to the first issue of Review Tales book magazine celebrating the best literary work. I want to thank everyone who contributed and helped make this happen.

We have come a long way from the traditional methods of publishing, writing, and marketing books. Independent authors genuinely need our help. Although their quality of writing and storytelling may be just as good as the authors who get signed, they still don't get the same credit, book deal, or recognition.

For this reason, the magazine is for everyone but especially for indie authors, providing them an opportunity allowing them to feel seen and heard.

In this issue, we begin with authors confessing about their journey, writing, publishing, and learning things they would have preferred to know beforehand. We then follow with ten book reviews and three author spotlights presenting outstanding works of literature.

Next, we unveil a list of selected books we think you should read in 2022. As the pandemic continued to be a source of stress, books proved to be the popular choice for relaxing and passing the time. For this reason, there has been a massive growth of sales in printed books, and as more people read books, what better way to provide an insightful source to read, enjoy and learn from. Happy Reading.

Jeyran Main

Founder & Editor-in-chief
Review Tales Magazine - Publishing - Editing Services

Author Confessions

Authors pour their hearts out, revealing the truth about their journey, providing tips and guidance on matters they'd prefer to have known. We hear authors give their best advice, discuss their writing process, mistakes they made, and things they preferred to know beforehand. It is time to confess!

Contributors

Rod A. Walters, Craig Deegan, Steven Day, and Dennis Scheel

"We are all apprentices in a craft where no one ever becomes a master."

—Ernest Hemingway

WHAT TO DO WHEN IT'S ALL NEW!
C A DEEGAN

Nowadays, getting your book published with the various tools and platforms available is easy if you aren't one of the 0.001% of authors to get a traditional publishing deal. But don't think that because you've published on the 'Zon', there will be crowds of people flocking to buy your opus magnum. You need to get it out there, and that's going to be down to you unless you can afford to employ a marketing guru to do it for you. So, here are my tips as someone who has trodden that well-worn path myself.

Cover

Get yourself a great cover! It's the first thing that will catch someone's eye and make them stop. If you can afford it, have someone experienced to do this for you; they are generally around USD 200, but you can pick up a pre-made one for a lot less. Do NOT scrimp on the cover. It's the key that opens the door to a new reader.

Blurb

If someone likes the cover, they will want to know more. Make sure your blurb gives enough to pique their interest but isn't too wordy. If you give away the whole story here, there is no point in them reading it. And don't plaster your reviews all over it; one is fine, but don't add more than that. People like to make up their own minds.

Price

You need to be realistic here as an unknown. People will give a new author a chance if it's not too expensive. Ebooks are great here, as they can be priced pretty low. I have seen new indie authors pricing their first book in the USD 20 range. It will have to be something pretty special to command that price, particularly for the fiction market. Keep it low to start.

Marketing

The 'M' word! Regardless of whether you have a book deal with a publisher or an indie publisher, you will have to market your book. If it's unknown, nobody is going to read it. Cheap ways to start marketing are:

- Book bloggers. But be nice; try to build a relationship with them first. Introduce yourself and tell them why you think they may like your book. And offer them a copy free of charge. These guys are inundated with requests, so you need to stand out.

· Social Media. You will need to get to grips with all the platforms; specific genres sell better in some than others. Instagram and Tiktok are best for younger markets, Facebook and Twitter for older ones. And don't just post in the huge "promote your book" here ones; they are full of authors doing the same. You need to find the groups for your genre and ask them.

· Adverts. Get to grips with Amazon and Facebook adverts! There are plenty of training videos out there to help.

You can do many more things, but this article is really a taster. If you have any questions, I'd be happy to try and answer them directly. Get to it and have a blast whilst you do!

C A Deegan lives in the East Midlands, right in the centre of the UK, and when he's not writing or working, he's with the family or walking the dog in the local woodlands seeking those ever-elusive Fae. "The Cracklock Saga" series of books came about from reading some pretty awful fairy books to his daughter over the years – she's in her teens now and has now (with more than a bit of relief!) left those behind. But as he ploughed through them with gritted teeth, he always wondered what would happen if someone didn't like fairies, what they would do about it, and could anybody stop them? This idea grew, and the Cracklocks were born. C A Deegan liked the idea of people who hated the Fae and everything they stood for. And who knew just how wicked those people were? He certainly didn't until Anastasia and Agatha got their claws in!

Book Title: Fae or Foe?
Pub Date: September 2021
ISBN: 978-1-739908-10-2
Book Category/Genre: Fantasy, Young Adult / Adult
Page Count: 359
Publisher: Self-published

WHAT DO YOU DO WITH A DRUNK-EN WRIT-ER'S BLOCK?
ROD A. WALTERS

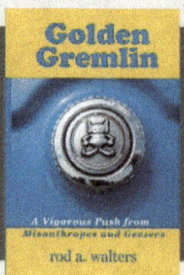

Writer's Block is worse than that "drunk-en sail-or" in the song. Cops can tuck the whiskied sailor away overnight, but writer's Block sticks closer than "mud on a hog's butt" (as they say on the farm). Right? With or without the whiskey.

What about all those great advice tidbits "out there" on un-blocking a writer's brain? A few will work, most won't. With one-third of my book to finish, and the other two-thirds wandering around disorganized, I took the drastic step of setting up a small personal board of advisors (PBOA) to get some rough-handed guidance.

After recovering from laughter at my being advised about this odd idea, I recalled Samuel Johnson's quip, "When a man knows he is to be hanged in a fortnight, it concentrates his mind wonderfully." Or something like that. A PBOA will concentrate the mind exceedingly well and hurts less than a hanging. Now, what is this PBOA all about? How did I "do" one?

I found these steps crucial:

- Pick a half dozen diverse-minded persons who can advise, not those who simply like me. Three to five board members work nicely.
- To start, send out detailed invitations to three. Not all will likely accept.
- "Pay" them. Professionals are more serious than amateurs. I chose to send each a $50 gift card of their choice. Require this payment step. No exceptions.
- Set a term for the board. I chose a one-year period to publish, consisting of four board meeting dates of one hour each. These had to be virtual, as members live in different cities.
- Compose an agenda and send that out well before the sessions; send follow-up notes afterward.
- Thank these good board members profusely a couple of times during all this and always after board sessions. A small gift or token would be a great idea.

Does a PBOA work? For me, yep!! Not only has board guidance been mind-concentrating, but the stubborn book got retitled and reorganized, and I have a brisk production schedule to finish—or else. So far, no hanging is necessary. No writer's blockhead either; just get the book done!

Rod A. Walters, a writing name, was a U.S. Army officer, then a corporate mechanical and chemical engineer, and now he writes. He doesn't know if he likes writing all that much, but he keeps doing it and will not stop. His pronouns are he, him, hey-you, and jackass. Currently, he lives in Rochester, New York, and keeps trying to keep pen ready, mind open, and mouth shut.

From GOLDEN GREMLIN, you will learn all kinds of useful tidbits (and bigbits) about how the world really runs, or at least how so much of it got messed up, e.g.:
- NATURE: boys, dogpoop, and carbon footprints.
- WORDS: the real meaning of Caucasian.
- BUSINESS: stakeholders, esp. through the heart.
- KITCHENS: cooking up tasty Dollar Store kale.
- HISTORY: how Hell froze, & how Earth Day got born.
- Golden boy gets to be GOLDEN GREMLIN.
- Seasonally warm gremlin songs. Sort of.

All this with a little Einstein, Richard Nixon, Pocahontas and Ben Stein mixed in. What more could you want!

Book Title: Golden Gremlin: A Vigorous Push from Misanthropes and Geezers
Pub Date: June 2016
ISBN: 978-0-984179-20-6
Book Category/Genre: Non fiction, Humor
Page Count: 232
Publisher: Omega Man Press

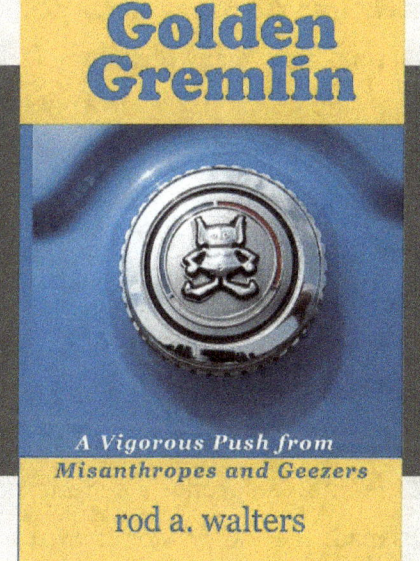

AUTHOR CONFESSIONS
DENNIS SCHEEL

When I was around eight years old, I discovered my interest in story-telling. Over the years, I ideated countless tales, filling my head with characters and plots. My ideas were omnipresent in my mind, but all my attempts to write them always ended after several pages.

Everything changed when I had a hypoglycemia (low blood sugar) attack. I'd endured minor attacks before due to diabetes, but this one was severe. I collapsed, and my dog barked louder than ever before to get anyone's attention. Someone called an ambulance for me, and when I woke up in the hospital, I was completely mute and paralyzed on my right side. After a few days, I started to regain my voice; the rest of my recovery was slower. A little over a month passed before I had movement in my fingers again.

After a year of physical therapy, I chose to try something new since so much had changed after my 'incident.' I started another attempt at writing my stories. My hopes were low, as I'd tried writing my stories many times before, but I wanted to try. All my previous attempts were in my first language (Danish), but the stories in my head had always played out in English. It was only natural that I gave English a chance. With these life changes, I finally managed to finish my first novel.

Curiously, the tale I had imagined since childhood wasn't the same on paper. The initial draft of my first novel stood at 107,000 words, but the editing process reduced it to 80,000 words. Despite this adjustment, it filled me with pride.

The next book in my series was a darker narrative and the ex who broke up with me after my incident inspired a character, a demon, Maia. Many of her characteristics fit the character, which helped me resolve any remaining feelings I had while also improving the plot. As dreadful as that relationship was, it helped give my story more meaning than initially anticipated.

The third story featured a part of the tale that I had intended from the very start, and I was excited to get it down on paper. The unexpected long story interweaves the distant past and the present day to create a tale of self-reflection.

As it turned out, I found my vision changing as I worked on my three novels, but some portion of them was already in my head when I started each one. While writing them, I actively saw how certain parts deviated from my original concept.

In the end, I found my way with my writing. Years of failed attempts and an experience that let me put life into perspective aided me along my authorial path, but I wouldn't trade any of it. These trials made me and my stories what we are today.

Dennis Scheel has always had stories running in his head but could not tell them until after his accident, which left him mute and paralyzed on his right side. After he worked his way back through recovery, he wanted to try to tell his story once more after an acquaintance told him he was talented at writing poetry. Before that, his ex-had convinced him not to write for ten years by insisting that he had no aptitude for writing. This time, Dennis tried writing his stories in English for the first time. Finally, he succeeded and has never stopped writing since. The effort has produced three stellar novels:

No Way Back- The Underworlds
Taken With a Dark Desire: The Underworlds
Rejecting Destiny: The Underworlds

Book Title: Rejecting Destiny: The Underworlds
Pub Date: August 2020
ISBN: 978-1-732429-04-8 (paperback)
　　　173-2-429-04-9 (e-book)
Book Category/Genre: Dark Fantasy, Science Fiction
Page Count: 774
Publisher: Self-published

OF POLITICS AND FICTION
STEVEN DAY

The Patriot's Grill, my debut novel, isn't just a little political. It reeks of the stuff. And I'm not talking about the enjoyable fluff which often passes as political fiction, thriller novels are written with a political backdrop. Perhaps the story of a president who personally dispatches a group of terrorists right after wrestling an alligator into submission on the wing of an airplane while in flight. The Patriot's Grill is political in a more intrusive sense, questioning the ongoing viability of our democracy.

In writing the book, I tried to avoid being melodramatic, or worse yet, overly preachy. I also made certain the story, not the politics, would always come first, but political overtones were never far behind.

The Patriot's Grill begins in 2099. America has been controlled by a brutal dictatorship for 70 years. Democracy and personal freedom aren't just dead. The dictatorship, in conjunction with its corporate and religious partners, has erased them from history. For Joe Carlton, bartender at The Patriot's Grill, such concepts are unimaginable. He's experienced nothing like them. But then an old man, with an unbelievable story, wanders into the Grill, and Joe's universe changes forever.

As important as the book's political message was to me, it was far from the only thing I cared about. I had the usual dreams of commercial success — delusions of grandeur, one might say.

But injecting politics into fiction carries a price. My Amazon customer rating unquestionably went down due to political disagreements. There were also a couple of nasty reader reviews. One called me a communist. My writing has about as much kinship to communism as banana pudding has to the spiciness of cayenne pepper, but such reactions are inevitable.

So why jump into this swamp when you're already facing the monumental challenge of trying to break through as a new writer? There's one good reason only — which is because you feel so strongly about something, silence isn't an option. For me, fear that American democracy is dying has been such an obsession, something which was already true in 1996, when I wrote the short story which later became the inspiration for The Patriot's Grill. Extreme economic inequality was just beginning then to be discussed outside of expert circles. The threat it posed to democracy seemed obvious. The economic disparity would invariably result in the super-wealthy gaining greater political power. That power would, in turn, allow them to amass even greater wealth, as they used their advantages to stack the economic deck.

More money would mean even more political power, allowing them to game the system in ways that would make their power unassailable. Popular disaffection with the resulting failure of democracy to meet the needs of average people would deepen and ultimately be redirected into tolerance for totalitarian leadership and hatred directed against scapegoats, such as immigrants.

Democracy would die, not in a volley of artillery fire, but in the slow rot of despair.

As the years passed, each step of this highly choreographed dance seemed to fall neatly into place. And with it, the corruption of the soul of American democracy grew deeper. What had started as an amateur guess about the future, was looking more like destiny. And it was then I knew, I had to write this book.

I wasn't naïve. A self-published book was unlikely to sell widely.

But I still had to write it.

Steven Day is a lawyer in Wichita Kansas. He has many "honors" as a lawyer and is the author of The Patriot's Grill.

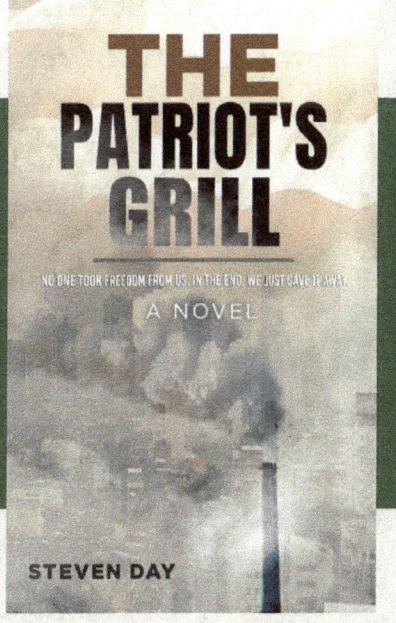

Book Title: The Patriot's Grill
Pub Date: August 2020
ISBN: 979-8-676198-22-0
Book Category/Genre: Thriller/Political, Science Fiction, Dystopian
Page Count: 324
Publisher: Self-published

TEN
Book REVIEW TALES Reviews

Review Tales is proud to have completed over 1100 book reviews so far. It is safe to say that we have seen our fair share of manuscripts. Our reviews have always been unbiased and constructive. We aim to help authors realize their strengths and encourage them to continue writing. 10 book reviews have been selected for this Winter issue.

TO APPLY FOR A BOOK REVIEW VISIT
WWW.JEYRANMAIN.COM

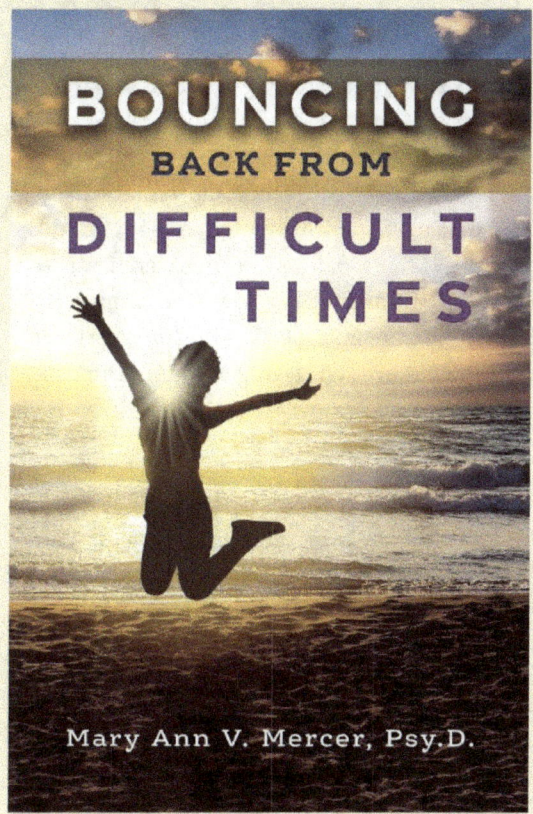

Mary Ann V. Mercer, Psy.D., is a Psychologist, Speaker & Intensive Coaching™ co-creator. Dr. Mercer co-authored many books, including SPONTANEOUS OPTIMISM™. She appears on TV & Radio, including Oprah, Home & Family, plus Crook & Chase. She delivers speeches & workshops and co-founded the self-help website www.PositiveLifeAnswers.com

Pub Date: August 2021
ISBN: 978-0-983273-98-1 (paperback)
       978-0-983273-96-7 (e-book)
Book Category/Genre: Self-help, Self-improvement
Pages: 145
Publisher: Bookbaby

Reviewer: Jeyran Main

Bouncing Back from Difficult Times
Mary Ann V. Mercer, Psy.D.

Bouncing Back from Difficult Times is a self-help book geared towards those who struggle with difficult times and find it tough to stick through them. This book makes an excellent attempt to explain why we feel this way and provides beneficial response patterns that help you move forward.

The author teaches you how to transform your discouraging beliefs into useful ones. You are encouraged to seek a hopeful life and pinpoint what you want and create what you desire.

The other important fact about this book is that the author does not just ask you to go and seek happiness. She coaches you using steps, methods, techniques, and setting achievable goals.

I recommend this book to those who wish to change their energy and vibrations mainly to change their life.

Radhika Iyer was born in Malaysia to migrant Indian parents and has lived in Malaysia, England, Dubai, and Ireland. She started writing short stories when she was studying in England more than 30 years ago. Her stories were on the winning list of the Malaysian NST-SHELL Short Story competition for two consecutive years in the early 1990s. Both stories were featured in the national newspaper and one story, The Unmarried Widow, was published in a mixed collection of short stories in 1991. Radhika currently lives in and is trying to fit into Dundalk, Ireland

Pub Date: August 2021
ISBN: 978-1-527291-38-6
Book Category/Genre: Contemporary Woman's Fiction
Pages: 67
Publisher: Castles in the Air Press

Reviewer: Jeyran Main

Why Are You Here?
Radhika Iyer

Why Are You Here? - is a collection of twelve short stories written with female narratives. The author's selection of storytelling demonstrates the struggles women face in different cultures and difficult circumstances.

The book does not shy away from discussing essential matters like rejection, abuse, racism, stereotyping, domestic violence, sexual abuse, and more.

I particularly enjoyed how the author's back story validated the one she has written. Radhika was born in Malaysia, and being the daughter of an immigrant, they were classed as a minority within a minority. This alone isolated her and led her to an even more complicated life, struggling with her identity and other mental issues.

I recommend this book to short story readers and those who enjoy understanding certain things women have to face.

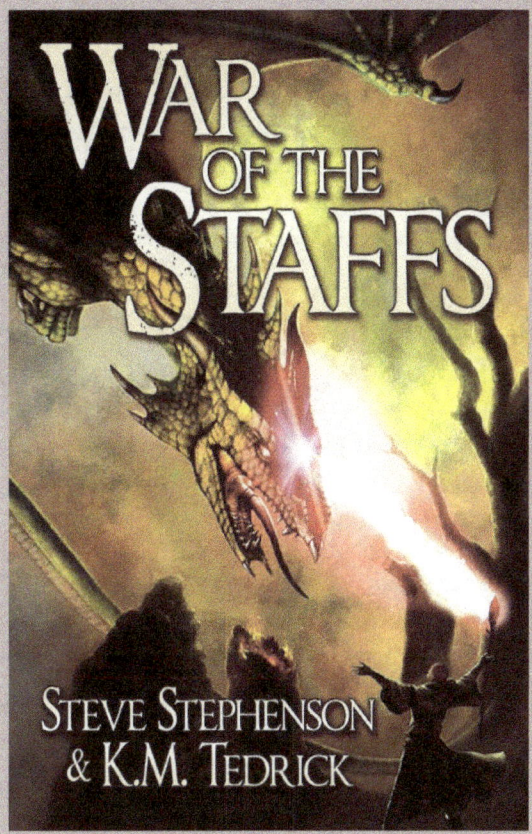

Kathryn Tedrick is a writer and ghostwriter in the fantasy, science fiction, Christian, and young adult genres. She has over thirty books published as a ghostwriter, four others as a co-author, and one book made into a movie. Steve Stephenson has written four books in the War of the Staffs fantasy series. He has a BA in History from the College of Charleston and an MA in Library Science from the University of South Carolina

Pub Date: July 2016
ISBN: 978-1-512967-17-2
Book Category/Genre: Epic Fantasy
Pages: 363
Publisher: Black Rose Writing

Reviewer: Jeyran Main

War of the Staffs
Steve Stephenson and K.M. Tedrick

War of the Staffs is an epic fantasy story. The story is set in a world called Muiria. A powerful vampire wizard, Taza has brought a vengeful goddess, Adois, through the void, a space between the planets, and lends him a powerful staff, simply intended to take over the planet and turn it from good to evil.

This is the first book of its series, and therefore you expect many character introductions. The story is filled with many villains. The imaginative setting is a treasure for those who love fantasy elements. If you're looking for dangerous, all-out battles including dragons, wizards, and more, then this book would be a gem for you.

The story's pace is slow, and the author has made sure there are enough sideline stories to expand on in the following books. The descriptive scenes and enjoyable tale keep you intrigued to read the story and want to know what will happen next.

I recommend this book to fantasy readers and those who like such world settings.

E. Prybylski is a writer, an editor, and a book publisher. She has been in the industry since around 2009, working first for Divertir Publishing and then for Insomnia Publishing. In addition to her work with them, she does freelance work. E. is a TTRPG enthusiast, historical reenactor (SCAdian), musician, cat mom, and avid gamer.

Pub Date: January 2022
ISBN: 978-1-734430-56-1 (paperback)
        978-1-734430-57-8 (e-book)
Book Category/Genre: Urban Fantasy
Pages: 168
Publisher: Insomnia Publishing

Reviewer: Jeyran Main

Fallen
E. Prybylski

Fallen is a fast-paced urban fantasy adventure story. It is the first book in the 'Smoke and Magic series.' The story begins with Cassiel, a fallen angel. She is taken to St. Mary's church to meet Father John, who is helping her understand who she is. When Father John is murdered, things change for Cassiel. With the help of her friends, she begins to piece together why this has happened and who it was.

Cassiel and her friends learn a few things in their search for answers. As the first book of its series, you get an excellent introduction to the characters and personalities. Some backstory blends well with the concept, and Cassiel's determination pulls everything together.

The literature is written well, and it is easy to envision the fantasy described. Not every part of the storyline gets closure, but what exists keeps the reader satisfied, wanting to know more. The premise was exciting and enjoyable to read.

I recommend this book to fantasy readers and demon lovers.

Very Far From Normal is Josie Allen's debut work. Although it was a transcription of journals kept at the time, most of it was written and edited around the fat cat in her lap. Josie Allen is a mother, a teacher, an actor, and a singer. She reads a lot. No really, a lot! She also designs and builds professional ballet tutus and makes cupcakes to die for!

Pub Date: July 2021
ASIN: B09B15SR7N
Book Category/Genre: Memoir, Non-fiction
Pages: 320
Publisher: Cottage Porch Press

Reviewer: Jeyran Main

Very Far From Normal: The real journals of a wife betrayed
Josie Allen

Very Far from Normal is a memoir written by Josie Allen, pouring her heart out and sharing her story in an honest and healing way. Josie and Sam were living a normal married life, but when Sam's secrets began to surface, things changed for the both of them.

The special thing about this book is that Josie does not entirely write this memoir for the purpose of telling it. She wrote it, making sure that even if that one person, going through the same thing, happened to come across this memoir, they too would not feel alone.

The story is about survival and focuses on a woman's strength and how much she can rely on herself to live through problems. It is most enjoyable to read but even more to inspire from.

I recommend this book to memoir readers and those who like to read a story about betrayal, love and family.

Dovydas Klimavičius is a Unique self-improvement book author, sleep expert, and an AI researcher.

Pub Date: September 2021
ASIN: B09H311CQ3
Book Category/Genre: Self-help, Self-improvement
Pages: 73
Publisher: Self-published via KDP

Reviewer: Jeyran Main

Diving Deeper Inside
Dovydas Klimavičius

Diving Deeper Inside is a self-help book geared for those who wish to understand willpower and comprehend the conscious and subconscious mind. The author discusses the importance of mindfulness and how effective it can be to overcome complex problems and reach personal growth.

The book can be used as a guide in teaching you about your mind and how to deal with your body benefiting you from making the right choices. We all somehow suffer from a lack of motivation and start something and fail after a few weeks.

I particularly enjoyed how the book teaches you to use your emotions and customize them to your advantage. You could do this with any goal you have in life, losing weight, gaining confidence, bettering your relationships, etc. Use fear to create excitement, or instead of suffering every day, enjoy the effort you put in. "Willpower is limited and limiting." We can't base anything on something that is limited. I recommend this book to those who want to learn about the mechanism of the human being and its complexities.

Reviewer: Jeyran Main

John was raised in an area of farms and abandoned ore mines in upper New York State where he came to know dowsers who could find water with a branch from a tree and a lady who could see auras and read palms and tea leaves with amazing accuracy.

He has always felt that there was more to our reality than that which science would allow. So, after college when he decided to 'put pen to paper,' he drew upon those people and stories to write "The Years of Magic" and "The Special Place," a supernatural comedy named "The Devil May Care" and, more recently, "The Witch's Song." Some of his stories have won awards and received good reviews. He still resides in that now not-so-rural community with his wife, JoAnn, and my dog, Mr. Biggie.

Pub Date: July 2021
ASIN: B09BBKJ6QH
Book Category/Genre: Coming of Age, Fantasy
Pages: 301
Publisher: Self-published

The Witch's Song
J. Lyndon Hickman

The Witch's Song is a young adult contemporary fantasy story about Claire and Crystal aged 21 and 18. They are poor, always on the move, and living with a man they believe is their father. The story is mostly about how Claire overcomes her emotional wounds growing up, dealing with the loss of her mother and being a witch.

The cover design is undoubtedly the first thing that grabs your attention. It is apparent that the author has taken time to make sure every detail has been given in publishing the book. The story is told well, and as you read along, you begin to feel a connection with the characters. Claire's personality, in particular, meshed well with the story. She was strong and someone you could relate to.

The girl's aunt, Carol, and her involvement with Claire taking her to the magical town of Elegy answers many of Claire's questions. This expanded the storyline. The literature and descriptive writing animated the impression of how every scene was taking place. This made the writing style suitable for the young adult audience and added to its appeal. I recommend this book to anyone who likes to read epic fantasy stories.

Bellwether, in partnership with the Ohio Writers Association, produces the Best of Ohio Short Stories anthologies and other fine work by Ohio authors. Callahan, Curtis A. Deeter, Carnegie Euclid, Dan Fogler, Joe Graves, Kirsta Hilton, Brian R. Johnson, Emily E. Jones, Stephen Kaczmarek, Stella Ling, Brian Luke, Elora Lyons, Mary McFarland, D. Wayne Moore, Devon Ortega, George Pallas, Brad Pauquette, Mike Sieminski, David M. Simon, and Steven Kenneth Smith.

Pub Date: October 2021
ISBN: 978-1-633375-46-8 (paperback),
978-1-633375-47-5 (e-book)
Book Category/Genre: Contemporary Fiction, Sci-fi, Fantasy
Page Count: 277
Publisher: Bellwether Publishing

Reviewer: Jeyran Main

Outcasts: An Anthology
Foreward by Dan Fogler

Outcasts is an anthology of eighteen short stories that showcase the skills of many authors' storytelling abilities. You notice the difference, change in conversation, and the diverse elements of character introductions within the premise as you read along.

The book's title stands out and makes you ponder how being an outcast can be a positive thing. Although the first few pages really begin to introduce what you may be expecting for the rest of the adventure, each story does stand alone and encourages you to read along.

The book is filled with humor, magical and nonmagical characters, and the writing is outstanding. It is an entertaining read, and I recommend it to those who like to read classic and captivating short stories.

Denver, Colorado, 2009. Nicholas Smith is done with the world. After losing his wife in Operation Iraqi Freedom, the devastated engineering professor sees only one way to escape his grief. But when he leaps from a waterfall into the waiting arms of oblivion, the haunted man of science instead finds himself impossibly catapulted into the year 3010.

Tortured at the hands of a despotic dictator, Nicholas refuses to cooperate despite being threatened with execution. After a desperate band of freedom fighters rescues him, the lost academic believes he may, at last, have found a reason to live. Can one man from the past bring hope to the future?

Exertions of Better Men is the thrilling first book in the Better Men science fiction series. If you like unexpected heroism, historical weaponry, and vividly evocative settings, then you'll love Ashley B. Venenga's apocalyptic what-if.

Pub Date: April, 2021
ISBN: 979-8-713976-61-3
Book Category/Genre: Science Fiction / Time Travel
Page Count: 256
Publisher: Amber Dragonfly LLC

Reviewer: Jeyran Main

Exertions of Better Men

Ashley B. Venenga

Exertions of Better Men is a time travel fiction story. It is set in a post-apocalyptic science fiction world and begins with Nicholas Smith, a college engineering professor living in Colorado. He learns that his wife passed away in Operation Iraqi Freedom and goes into a deep depression, wanting to end his life. When he jumps from the Holy Falls, where he married his then-wife, he wakes up in an entirely different environment. He has landed in the year 3010.

Nicholas has to start everything anew with a different purpose in life. His character growth and how he deals with his situation were interesting to read. Things are not easy for him, and he definitely faces some dramatic ups and downs.

The story is intense and action-packed. I found the premise to be novel and recommend this book to those who read time travel stories.

In addition to being a novelist, Rob Samborn is a screenwriter, entrepreneur, and avid traveler. He's been to forty countries, lived in five of them, and studied nine languages. As a restless spirit who can't remember the last time he was bored, Rob is on a quest to explore the intricacies of our world and try his hand at a multitude of crafts; he's also an accomplished artist and musician, as well as a budding furniture maker. A native New Yorker who lived in Los Angeles for twenty years, he now makes his home in Denver with his wife, daughter, and dog.

For more information visit http://www.robsamborn.com.

Pub Date: November 2021
ISBN: 978-1-952816-89-5
Book Category/Genre: Thriller, Historical Fiction, Magical Realism
Pages: 333
Publisher: TouchPoint Press

Reviewer: Jeyran Main

The Prisoner of Paradise
Rob Samborn

The Prisoner of Paradise is a historical fiction thriller about Nick taking a trip to Venice only to collapse after hearing a voice from Tintoretto's Paradise, a monumental depiction of Heaven. Although his wife asks him to seek help, Nick realizes that his blackout has sent him back to the 16th century, meeting Isabella Scalfini, an aristocrat that he was tasked to seduce but instead fell in love with.

The dynamic of the story then explains how Nick is totally lost in his hallucination only to realize that he has to make a wrong right before he can live the life he is currently in. The thriller story teaches you about Venetian history, art, and its social mores.

The story blends the past with the future in a way that your heart emerges from each scene, entering another one without hesitation. It is a tale worth reading, and if the book cover hasn't convinced you yet, then the premise should. I recommend this book to magic realm readers and historical fiction fans.

Words of Wisdom

Wisdom is the quality of having experience, knowledge, and good judgment. As writers journey through the publishing process, they gain an immense amount of wisdom worth sharing. We are honored to have a selection of their thoughts and insight with this segment of "Words of Wisdom."

Contributors

Boshra Rasti, Robert Bossler, Rob Samborn, George Pallas, Rojé Augustin, Brett Atlas, Louise Bélanger

"To defend what you've written is a sign that you are alive."

—William Zinsser, WD

PIERCING WORDS
BOSHRA RASTI

Writing must pierce. Being a writer is like sitting on the table for your first tattoo, earring, or nose ring. It is like the searing needle burning into your skin; the drop of blood is the symbol of what you've done. Your body is forever altered.

And the way the world sees you has also changed. You've made an impression on it; on every passerby that briefly or profoundly stares at you. The gaze depends on the beholder. For some, it's the spectacle of a freak. For others, an attractive impression burned into their mind. It doesn't matter what the reader sees; it matters that the writer has become vulnerable to the gaze of others.

That's what scares me about a world without creative spectacle, a needle and a body. The world in question may very well be dystopian. Seemingly harmonious rules and order ruled it, but that's what cuts the body's nose despite its face.

Writing and art push the boundaries. Creating the I am, and You are essential to the disgusting or adoring gaze of the other. From that place, society can learn tolerance, understanding, and progress.

Without creativity, we are doomed to our own banality and flattening. In my novel, Surrogate Colony, people are given X-ray vision to protect themselves from viruses and bacteria. However, X-ray vision in Microscrep isn't meant to create the piercing reality that society needs to be vulnerable or creative. It is used to control the chaos collectively. However, as the main character, Adriana learns, we cannot have creativity or desire without chaos.

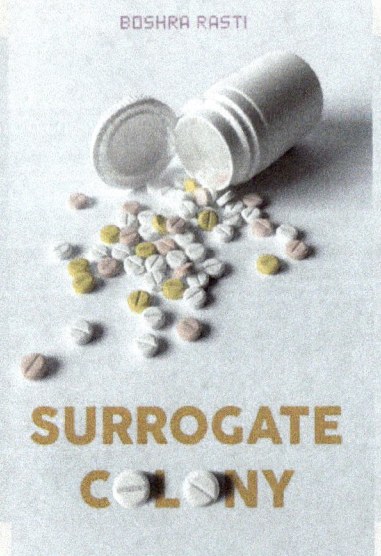

Book Title: Surrogate Colony
Pub Date: Feb 2022
ISBN: 978-1-639881-62-8
Book Category/Genre: YA, Sci-Fi: Dystopian
Page Count: 267
Publisher: Atmosphere Press

WORDS OF WISDOM
ROJÉ AUGUSTIN

Some years ago, I came across an axiom often proclaimed in the black community, which states that black folks have to be twice as good just to be good enough. What I understood this to mean was that we had to shine so brightly; ignoring the brilliance would be an egregious act of discrimination. I was in my early twenties when I read this, and something about it resonated deeply. I decided from then on that if I wanted equal opportunity, I would need to live my life in such a way that would bring me as close to twice as good as possible. So I became very focused: I got educated, got healthy, and got spiritual. I committed myself to a life of expansion, compassion, integrity, and love.

Now when I take stock, two important lessons emerge from trying to be 'twice as good.' One is the obstacles I've had to overcome, which turned out to be blessings in disguise. Obstacles are like whetstones; the kind used to sharpen knives. A whetstone must be hard and unyielding if it is to sharpen a blade. Without it, the blade becomes dull and useless over time. In a sense, you could say that whetstones are to knives what obstacles are to individuals — the harder the whetstone, the sharper the knife; the greater the obstacle, the stronger we become, particularly if we can face those obstacles with gratitude.

This brings me to the second important lesson — giving thanks. Gratitude, I have come to learn, is like a divine loophole. It brings a certain purity into any moment, a purity that can transform a rotten situation into gold. No matter what it is. One doesn't necessarily have to believe it. All that's required is that one expresses it: I give thanks. Such a simple thing, and yet it has transformed my life.

So if there are words of wisdom I can impart, it is to always give thanks for the obstacles. They are the hard, unyielding whetstones on which we sharpen ourselves.

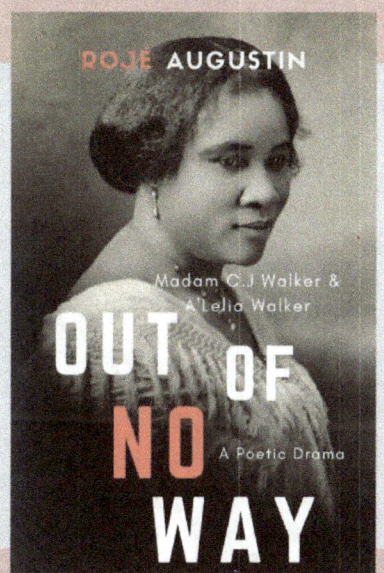

Book Title: Out of No Way: Madam C.J. Walker, a Poetic Drama
Pub Date: May 2020
ISBN: 978-0-987373-47-2
Book Category/Genre: Poetry, African American, Historical
Page Count: 156
Publisher: Boukman Press

FINDING YOUR AUDIENCE
LOUISE BÉLANGER

Writing poetry has become my passion. I have self-published two books so far, and I am working on my third one. Your Words and Your Words Your World are collections of inspirational poems accompanied by photography.

The biggest struggle for a new author is for our work to get noticed in a sea of books. It's easy to say: "You need to find your audience." Sure, but where and how?

I started with the popular social media platforms where readers and authors interact. A blogger read my book and posted their review, and a little domino effect occurred. I connected with authors, benefited from their experience, was introduced to other promotion sites, and learned how to expand the distribution of my books. You need to try different sites in order to find the one that works for you, as some may not be the right fit.

I recently started entering poetry contests. One of my poems will be published in an anthology in 2022. I took the time to celebrate. Other contests were less successful. Be willing to try new things, even if they don't always produce the result you'd hope for. In taking these risks, you gain experience, build confidence, and grow as an author.

I saw an online book blog tour featuring a different genre. I did some research and chose one that specializes in poetry. As I write this article, the tour is in full swing. More domino effects.

Stay encouraged by focusing on the reasons why you write. Getting readers, sales, followers, and an audience does take time, but if you enjoy the journey, you will not mind the wait.

Lastly, I've been a reader all my life. Before becoming an author, I rarely wrote book reviews. I didn't know the value of them then, but now I know better. I take time to write reviews because I believe in caring for others and helping the writing community.

May you find your audience; I'm slowly finding mine.

Book Title: Your Words Your World
Pub Date: July 2021
ISBN: 979-8-526756-09-9
Book Category/Genre: Inspirational & Religious Poetry
Page Count: 99
Publisher: Self-published

RELATING TO WONDER
ROBERT BOSSLER

What have I learned in my years of telling stories to children? Children have vivid, creative, and often extravagant imaginations. You can learn a lot about the kinds of stories that will interest a child by listening to those stories that the child likes to tell. Engaging children in play is fun, but it is also instructive and good practice.

Creating inspired stories for children requires an author to (re)connect with their own source of wild irreverence. Your story can be about anything; it can take your characters anywhere in the universe and beyond, and children will hang on your every word if you have a compelling narrative and relatable characters. But "relatable" is such a broad, encompassing concept, and it, too, can occur in the context of extravagant imagining. As long as they are well written, children can relate with dump trucks, giant bugs, old houses, and even slimy alien monsters from Planet Q. If your characters talk in language that children understand, if they act in ways familiar to a child's own actions and experiences, then children will be able to see themselves in any humdrum or ludicrous creation you place in front of them. For example, my latest book features talking animals, a depressed sun and is centered on the journey of a brave little star.

We might not always think it obvious, but this concept of being relatable extends to adults as well. As long as there is a glimmer of truth poking through all the wonderful, charming, disarming "lies" of a well-spun yarn, then readers of all ages will find meaning and relation with the story you are telling. For as long as humans have been telling stories, the truth behind the words resonates with the audience. The stories we remember best are the ones that tell us something about ourselves; remind us of something we sometimes forget. And the best children's stories are the ones that are not written to narrow the focus of the tale to children but instead to broaden the scope of relation to include children.

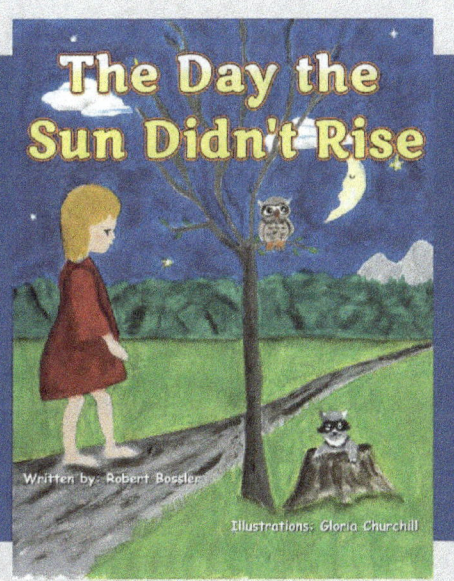

Book Title: The Day the Sun Didn't Rise
Pub Date: October 2021
ISBN: 979-8-482296-42-4
Book Category/Genre: Children's Literature
Page Count: 32
Publisher: Self-published

THINKING OUTSIDE THE BOX
ROB SAMBORN

To say authors are inundated with book marketing & publicity avenues is an understatement. As a debut novelist, I was thrown into the maelstrom head-first. From building a website to social media to advance reviews to press to well, you name it; I felt like I needed to take advantage of every possible opportunity. This left precious time to pursue my original marketing plan, which included out-of-the-box activities that are organic to the story.

THE PRISONER OF PARADISE (TouchPoint Press) is a thriller blended with historical fiction and fantasy, set in Venice, Italy, in the present-day and the 16th century. In the vein of Diana Gabaldon's Outlander and Dan Brown's Robert Langdon series, the book revolves around Paradise, the world's largest oil painting, completed in 1592 by Renaissance master Jacopo Tintoretto. The lead secondary character is a young emerging Venetian artist. Therefore, I've always wanted to market the book around art and Venice.

Of all the marketing, publicity, and promotions I'm doing, I'm more excited about this cross-promotion than any of them. The paintings will be exhibited at a gallery in Venice, and prints will be sold on my website and the artists' websites.

Of course, I hope that publicity from the art will lead to book sales, but I'm more excited about supporting these emerging artists. Hopefully, it will be a mutually beneficial relationship, and the book will lead to sales of their artwork. Beyond sales, there are additional ancillary benefits and opportunities, some already coming to fruition. For example, we're speaking with a major Venice-related non-profit about doing additional promotions or even an event. I encourage all authors to think outside the box and look to market their book in ways that are organic to the story. Have you already done similar marketing? Do you have out-of-the-box ideas?

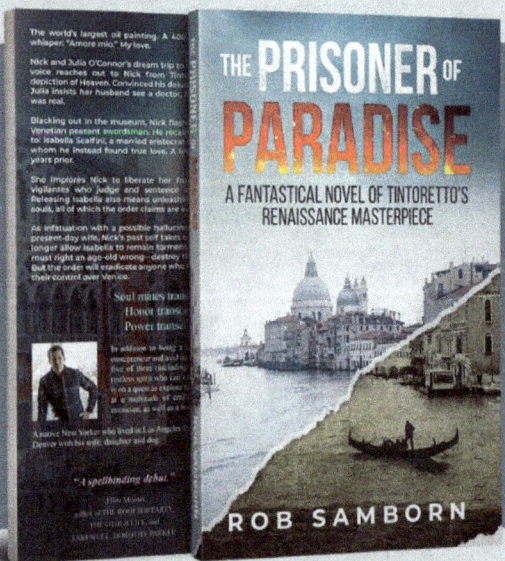

Book Title: The Prisoner of Paradise
Pub Date: November 2021
ASIN: B09F8RYG2M
Book Category/Genre: Historical Thriller
Page Count: 433
Publisher: TouchPoint Press

THE POWER OF YOUR PEERS
GEORGE PALLAS

Peer review is standard in academic circles. Having one's peers evaluate your work before publishing it is a way to ensure that arguments are sound and the evidence is solid. But did you know that a form of peer review can also help writers?

The Ohio Writers' Association, of which I'm a member, conducts workshops where writers can get feedback on their work from the workshop attendees. Before the workshop, attendees submit their writing, and the group reviews it. Submissions can be short stories, book chapters, or any other type of writing for review.

Our workshops have two simple rules. The first is that "feedback" is the reviewer's reaction to the material as a reader, not as a fellow writer. It is not advice or suggestions. A proper reaction would be something like, "I didn't understand why Joe did..." On the other hand, "You should include more about Joe's history of..." crosses over into giving advice. What you want is a reader's reaction, not how another writer might compose the story differently. In this way, the writer can learn where readers may see weak spots, but it is entirely up to him (or her) how to address the issue or if they feel it needs addressing at all.

The second rule is that writers receiving feedback must listen and not try to defend their work. If the piece needs an explanation, then there is something that will likely be unclear to potential readers. Those readers won't have the advantage of hearing explanations made during a peer review.

Participants in our workshops are all writers of varying degrees of experience. But what if you don't have easy access to other writers? Since the purpose of a peer review is to get readers' reactions, any group can peer-review your work. Nor does a peer review have to be a formal group. Try soliciting peer reviews and see how it will give you fresh insights into making your story or book better.

Book Title: Outcasts: An Anthology
Pub Date: October 2021
ISBN: 978-1-633375-46-8 (paperback)
978-1-633375-47-5 (e-book)
Book Category/Genre: Contemporary Fiction, Sci-fi, Fantasy
Page Count: 277
Publisher: Bellwether Publishing

CREATING SOMETHING MEANINGFUL
BRETT ATLAS

Every author has a first book. That's important to remember because many people do not believe they are qualified -or allowed- to create something meaningful. If you are a member of that group, I hope my story inspires you to sit down and free those powerful ideas swirling around in your head.

My dad was my hero, and I wanted to be just like him. Growing up, he always tried to teach me, share tidbits of wisdom, and roll out life's carpet one section at a time. Wherever a problem or challenge existed, I was certain my dad had the answer. I was once made aware of random letters he wrote to my brother. I sat at his desk over the years, occasionally envisioning a day when I would receive them as part of a compendium of valuable guidance.

When he passed away in 2015, I thought about those letters, and I anticipated receiving one more life lesson, one more piece of advice, one more thing he hadn't told me before. I never believed he'd leave this world without saying everything he wanted to say. But there were no letters, and I was left with a sunken, empty feeling. I envisioned my own kids in my place, and I was determined to teach them all the valuable life lessons I'd worked so hard to learn. I ended up writing them the book I wish I had when I was younger.

I had written several short articles at that point, but nothing like a full book. I wasn't famous or a motivational speaker, so I couldn't rely on a guaranteed audience. Frankly, If I had listened to some of the advice I received, I would have given up before starting. But I didn't waste energy worrying about whether anyone would publish it or buy it. What motivated me was creating something meaningful that I would be proud of. I focused only on accomplishing that goal.

There is a section in my book Three Things Matter, Most dedicated to the process of setting priorities. In it, I used the actual writing of the book as an example of how to break up large projects into small tasks. My dad used to remind me, "You know how you eat an elephant? One bite at a time." It took many bites over many months, but my book was finished, edited, and published. I can't fully describe the feeling of seeing my kids read it. Perhaps equally as thrilling as hearing other people buying additional copies for their own children to read.

You can't finish something you don't start, and you can't start unless you believe in yourself. We all have something meaningful inside us that is waiting to come out. Once you've given it a home, it will live forever on the page.

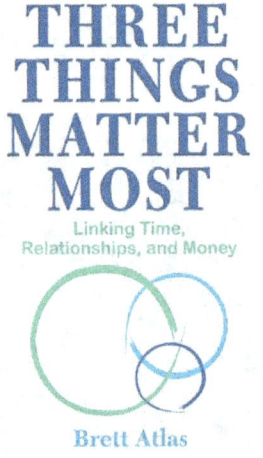

Book Title: Three Things Matter Most:
Linking Time, Relationships, and Money
Pub Date: September 2021
ISBN: 978-1-950091-54-6
Book Category/Genre: Self-help
Page Count: 219
Publisher: Addicus Books

Author Interview

From all over the world, we talk to authors about their creative process and inspirational journey. We appreciate their honesty and read through their personal experience.

Contributors

Siobhán O'Regan, Kate Peters, Caroline Clemens

"Don't tell me the moon is shining; show me the glint of light on broken glass."

—Anton Chekhov

Siobhán O'Regan
AUTHOR OF "NOBODY SPECIAL, FROM A TRAUMA

Author Interview

Where did you get your information or idea for your book?

The title was easy; I was never anyone's first, second, or even third growing up; the only attention I did get was usually violent and consistently hostile. I traced my story from the very beginning backing it all up with documents from various therapists, doctors, and institutions. In some cases, my younger sister could fill in the blanks for the pieces I couldn't remember myself.

When did you first realize you wanted to be a writer?

As a child, I had a passion for writing short stories and poems. I used to spend days, weeks, and months at a time as a prisoner in my room with nothing to keep my mind, body, and spirit busy. I had no books, no radio, nothing but a bed (which I was never allowed to use during the day), a dresser, and four walls. So, I used to steal pens from school. I would scribble on toilet paper and flush it down the toilet so I would escape getting caught. I lived inside my own head for many years. This became my reprieve and my release. I was in Trauma therapy for almost two years to overcome a severe attachment disorder in my early thirties. It was my therapist who suggested I write this book. This was the seed that bloomed into the work that I proudly share with you today.

What do you like to do when you're not writing?

I love to sing, dance like no one is watching, spend time with my dog Jack, my horse Kallan and hang out with my family. I have the most fabulous job working with at-risk youth, and I look forward to going to work every day. Sometimes I have so much fun; it hardly seems like work at all. I work with the most remarkable humans who recognize my strengths and enhance my life daily, and I pay it forward in kindness. We were foster parents for nine years. I ran a board for nine years, and I currently hold a volunteer community service worker position for a local non-profit organization. My amazing husband has been standing in line waiting for his turn to spend time with me, and I can't wait until we can focus on one another again.

As a child, what did you [want to be] when you grew [up]?

If I had the proper supports growing up, I wanted to be either a police officer or a dancer. Next to writing, I loved the art of dance, one of my fondest memories as a child was dancing to Staying Alive by the Bee Gees with my grandmother just months before she passed away. This memory has stuck with me throughout the years. To this day, I seldom watch television or movies. I am content to put on some music and dance to myself while cleaning, organizing, crafting, or playing with my furry companions.

What was one of the most surprising thing you learned in creating your book?

The most surprising thing I learned writing my book was how therapeutic it was and how much healing I did throughout the process. The entire reasoning behind my book was so I could help those who are justifiably lost and trying to find their way. I once told a therapist that I could be in a room full of people and still feel completely alone. He said it was because I wasn't among like-minded people and that there is strength in numbers.

From a trauma perspective, Nobody Special takes an in-depth look into the life of a young girl who was robbed of her childhood. She was ripped away from her siblings by the very system meant to protect her and written out of her grandfather's eulogy. To them, she no longer existed. She would grow up with a severe attachment disorder, complex PTSD, and develop Stockholm syndrome. She was only seven months when her abuse began.

This is a tale of survival, resiliency, and how she overcame the odds.

This book covers mental health disorders, concurrent disorders, addictions, genetic disorders, immune disorders, perspective, and healthier vs. unhealthy mindset.

Pub Date: August 2021
ISBN: 978-1-988680-08-8 (e-book)
       978-1-988680-09-5 (paperback)
Book Category/Genre: Memoirs
Page Count: 372
Publisher: Review Tales Editing & Publishing Services

Kate Peters
AUTHOR OF "FLASHES AND SPARKS"

Author Interview

Do you have a confession to make as an author?

I think most indie authors face this existential crisis, like, now what; will this work live on after I stop breathing my life into it? And that's what writing is—documenting living, even if that's just the life of the mind.

When did you realize you wanted to be a writer?

In high school, I wrote poetry—just like lots of new adults under the influence of ennui. But, I sought solace there in my free time. It energized me. I would encourage anyone to examine where they run when the things that they're required to do are done.

I think each one of us has innate gifts. When I was about fifteen, I found an old pocket watch in a box of family heirlooms. It was dated 1924, and the engraved inscription thanked my great grandmother for serving as President of the American Pen Women's Association. I was pleasantly surprised and shocked. But, not really, you know? By then, I knew I was not likely to become a mathematician, but this pocket watch whispered to me, and the writer in my genes started to listen.

There have also been teachers in my life who have reaffirmed my love of writing in one way or another. I'm a lawyer, so this is ironic, but my criminal law professor told me that my first-year exam was abysmal but well written and that "Maybe you're just a really great writer." (I assure any of my clients reading this that I nailed the final.)

It was my high school Honors English teacher who affirmatively encouraged my writing. He, an author, Mr. Littrell, would put these amazing poems and unusual words up on the board each day for us to just take in at the start of class. We'd marinate a moment in the poem, croon over the meaning of a unique word. Dennis's enthusiasm for written language continues to inspire me, and we still write to each other once in a while.

How do you schedule your life when you're writing?

I dream of the bohemian life, retreating to some ancient, off-the-grid town on a Greek isle and writing until the cicadas are quieted, and the sun goes down. Instead, I'm waking up in the dark and making breakfast, school lunches, and heading off to work. I began writing in earnest as a sort of revenge against this life, to do something that was just for me.

From a hot spot connection in the school pickup line to the waiting room at the dentist, I seek out solace in my days. But, I'm not always disciplined enough to write. I fall wildly into that spiral of how deserving I am of doing nothing, spending months of my free time seeking out quick entertainment on flashing screens. I try to remind myself that those screens speed uptime, and what I want to do is preserve it. When I'm on a treadmill, minutes are hours. Mental exercise also seems to slow downtime. So, the busier I am, the more I feel I need to write.

Pub Date: October 2020
ISBN: 978-1-735728-06-3
Book Category/Genre: Memoirs
Page Count: 250
Publisher: Warren Publishing

What was one of the most surprising things you learned in creating your book?

In addition to creating a world where all my efforts were just for me, I took my initial stab at writing a novel to see if I could really do it. What I learned is that anyone can do it.

It's like losing 100 pounds. Sounds nearly impossible, right? But, what about ten pounds, ten times? With discipline, it's possible. People do it. And, just as with a good character, a writer must have her why defined to achieve this kind of success. Why did they do it? Why would you spend your precious time writing? I don't think it's possible to write well if it's purely for others. This tremendous and solitary work must be equaled by tremendous joy.

I hear people say they'd love to write, but they don't have an interesting story to tell. I believe there is a story in just about anything if you're really paying attention, slowing down to the details. In that meditative state, writing about a snowflake becomes an exploration of a unique hexagonal ice formation falling through the atmosphere and colliding in clusters over space and time. No two flakes are exactly alike. And, none of us are exactly like the other. But, there are relatable points in all our lives that come in cycles, like the return of the full moon. A writer's goal is to illuminate our shared humanity, to strike when a theme has come full circle. This clarity in the darkness is where the story lies.

Caroline Clemens
AUTHOR OF "MAGENTA FLEURS"

Author Interview

How do you schedule your life when you're writing?

I write a lot. And it flows from me, and rarely do I have writer's block. I do it all alone with minimal help. I'm hoping to either have sales or a publisher believe in me and sell my material for streaming. That's the goal. I want to write for ten more years! I think I'm okay. Though, I do need more feedback. The singer that gets the audience didn't start off wanting the applause, but I think that's the icing on the cake, the crumpet with the tea, and the glass of wine with dinner.

How do you process and deal with negative book reviews?

I've had one or two negative reviews. Yes, they are bothersome. I read it to find out any useful information. Then I decided I would NEVER do that to any writer. The professional writers have loads of editors, etc., and the indie or self-published do it with little funds. I don't give less than three. That doesn't mean every three is a bad book. I don't publicly disgrace someone for trying their best. That's how I roll. If it isn't a three, I don't publish a review.

Where did you get your information or idea for your book?

I got the idea for the thriller books from my phone; you know that thing you clutch to on an hourly basis. Everyone has one, and do you know who is watching, listening and maybe altering your life? Scary, no, make that ultra-difficult! I fabricated details about several women who are being followed and monitored. But by who? This is an excellent concept-so don't steal my idea. The Snowden whistleblower made me think, and then I wrote whatever I could make up. The third book will envelop the series; then, I'll be onto another concept.

Kristan sets off to college and meets new friends amidst a whole new world. Simultaneously missing her mother, she embarks upon her future with classes, Shakespeare, sonnets, old loves and new friends. By Christmas break, her world takes a new direction, and with help from strangers, she meets a fate almost destined for this worldly young girl. Her friends Scarlet and Jeremy begin to date in Savannah while a trip to an island bears a story no one saw coming. How delightful!

This fiction reads with tragic elements, romance, and even cybercrime. A perfect summer read with the magic of emotional feels as your heart repeatedly reels again and again. A third book gets going in 2022.

Pub Date: May 2021
ISBN: 978-0-578906-98-0
Book Category/Genre: Thriller/Mystery Suspense
Page Count: 334
Publisher: IvoryTide Press

Follow Review Tales

 https://www.facebook.com/talesreview

 https://twitter.com/TalesReview

 https://www.facebook.com/groups/reviewtales

Editor's Pick

In this second book in the Real Life Series, you'll discover the reasons behind your self-doubt and lack of confidence. You'll read real life stories with examples and suggestions of how to overcome fear and negativity and, hopefully, you'll find a few answers to help guide you in the search for your personal truth.

Pub Date: April 2021
ISBN: 978-1-735860-72-5
Book Category/Genre: Self-help, Self-improvement, Personal Growth, Personal Development, Life Success
Page Count: 182
Publisher: Redstone Press

Ever since humans became self-aware, we have struggled to find the meaning of life. The price we paid for becoming intelligent was to become painfully ignorant of the difference between good and evil.
Humans have come a long way by questioning the nature of objects around us and pushing the limits of our intelligence, but it's now time that we ask the greatest question yet:
when does intelligence transcend to become consciousness?

Pub Date: April 2021
ISBN: 979-8-738415-82-1
Book Category/Genre: Philosophical Fiction
Page Count: 210
Publisher: Self-published

Beginning with his debut novel—A Cobbler's Tale, followed by Moon Flower, The Righteous One, The Bomb Squad, Hope City, Sadie's Sin, Cape Nome and soon to be released—Otzi's Odyssey, Neil Perry Gordon has established himself as a well-respected and prolific historical and metaphysical fiction novelist. His storytelling ability has earned him high editorial praise from the likes of Kirkus, Midwest Book Review and others, including hundreds of four and five star reader reviews on Amazon and Goodreads.

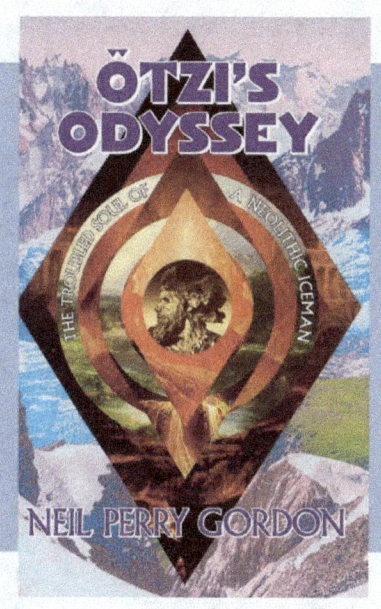

Pub Date: November 2021
ISBN: 978-1-732667-73-0
Book Category/Genre: Metaphysical fiction
Page Count: 291
Publisher: Self-published

The Vanishing Point is about disappearance, trauma, and memory, and the possibilities of redemption through a great American road trip and a peek into a mid-western childhood. It is a meditation on Karma and the way we lose and find ourselves over and over again.

Pub Date: September 2021
ISBN: 173-4-786-53-1
Book Category/Genre: Literary Fiction
Page Count: 371
Publisher: Cactus Moon Publications

Starred Books

High romance, pitched battles and titillating humor are featured in this retelling of a beloved fairy tale that chronicles the many adventures of Cinderella's prince as he experiences his first joust, undergoes his baptism of fire in the Battle of Paris, is charmed by Cinderella at a masquerade ball, and sets off on a quest to find her after she flees the ball at the midnight hour.

The quest takes him and his folksy mentor, Sir Guy, through strange lands supposedly inhabited by ogres, pixies, hobgoblins, man-eating plants and giants; and peopled by an extraordinary and motley cast of characters that include an epileptic bard, a bean counter who wagers his gold tooth in a dice game, a merchant who can never be too prosperous, a little girl who has a running feud with three bears, pilgrims that argue over who is the most pious and a beggar who has been cursed with leprosy for committing all the cardinal sins. Be on the look-out for a bit of Chaucer-like satire in this adapted fairy tale.

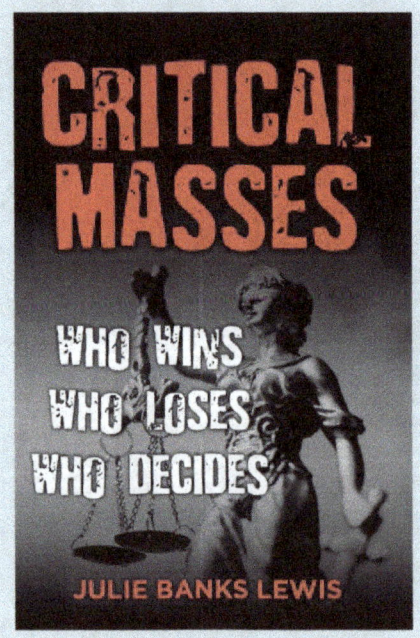

Critical Masses is a self-help, non-fiction book, and it assesses the power dynamics and structural inequalities throughout American history. It discusses the system or powers, capitalism, democracy, patriarchy, and so much more.

It was sad to see how the power elite are the ones who control the movement and fate of the living. I found it fascinating to know how schools, churches', propaganda, and strategic positioning affected gender equality, race, and ethnicity. It was evident to see why these topics have always created division amongst people. You can defiantly understand the term divide and conquer when you read this book.

An award-winning memoir, Ninety-Nine Fire Hoops is for anyone who has struggled with gender inequality, racism, and immigrant injustice. Ultimately, it's about a strong woman of color determined to create her own path.

Meet the Kenderleys, the wealthiest and most powerful family in the world.

The youngest, Prince Bonifaz, takes his lessons and trusts no one. The middle child, Princess Isabel, sneaks away to a secret regency of her own making. Their mother, Queen Dulcibella, watches out for her children just as readily as she watches over them. Their father, King Jonnecht, is a capricious tyrant who hopes to control his family as strictly as he does the largest empire, and his violent rage threatens all under his rule.

Then there's Prince Ewald, eldest and heir to the throne. No one is more aware of the threat his father poses to everyone. No one has better legal standing to do anything about it. How can he save everyone he loves while upholding his mother's kind values? He must learn the lessons required to be the best regent, choose allies wisely and earn their trust, and enact a thoughtful and detailed plan.

"Everybody is a genius. But if you judge a fish by its ability to climb a tree, it will live its whole life believing that it is stupid."

- ALBERT EINSTEIN

www.jeyranmain.com